This book belongs to:

May our house always be
too small to hold
all of our friends.

–Myrtle Reed

Gooseberry Patch
2500 Farmers Dr., #110
Columbus, OH 43235

www.gooseberrypatch.com
1·800·854·6673

Copyright 2011, Gooseberry Patch 978-1-936283-91-0
First Printing, May, 2011

All rights reserved. No part of this book may be reproduced or
utilized in any form or by any means, electronic or mechanical,
including photocopying and recording, or by any information
storage and retrieval system, without permission in
writing from the publisher. Printed in Korea.

Gooseberry Patch®

Tiny Tips
for
Get-Togethers

Dedication

To all those who know that combining food, friends and fun is always a winning recipe!

*Small cheer and great welcome
makes a merry feast.*

–William Shakespeare

At your next dinner party, set out a guest book!
Ask everyone young and old to sign...it will become
a treasured journal of the occasion.

Get out the craft supplies and make some fun placecards!
Encourage lively table conversation among guests
who don't know each other by writing names
on the backs of the cards as well as the fronts.

Serve meals on your very best china and linens today...no need to save them for a special occasion!

A can't-go-wrong mix of vintage and new tableware is always a fun and different way to serve up dinner...so go ahead and choose all your favorites.

Platters of food set on different levels make
a more interesting presentation. Use books, a stack
of plates or upside-down pots and bowls on a buffet
table to create different heights. Simply cover with
a tablecloth and set serving dishes on top!

Delight the whole gang by having an appetizer party!
Serve four to five different dishes and guests can
choose their favorites.

A good rule of thumb for appetizers...serve 6 to 8 per person if dinner will follow. Plan for 12 to 15 per person if it's an appetizer-only gathering.

Slow cookers are perfect party helpers!
Just plug them in and they'll keep food bubbly and yummy with no effort at all.

Background music adds to everyone's enjoyment at a party. Ask at a nearby school to find a music student who would be willing to play piano, guitar or violin for a modest fee, or visit your local library and borrow some CDs of jazz, salsa or pop tunes.

It's a lovely thing...everyone sitting down together, sharing food.

–Alice May Brock

Add some western flair to your next outdoor gathering for instant fun!

Drape a big blanket on the picnic table, serve sandwiches on graniteware plates and wrap the flatware in big squares of burlap or bandannas tied with roping.

Fill Mason jars with cool water and cheery bouquets...a perfect fit tucked inside cowboy boots!

You're never too old for party favors!
Send your guests home with a whimsical
memento...tiny potted plants, little bags of
homemade candy, mini photo frames
or even bubbles.

One cannot have too large a party.

–Jane Austen

Warm up dinner with friends by hosting a casual fireside supper. Toast sandwiches in pie irons and make s'mores for dessert...so cozy!

Toss a bundle of cinnamon sticks or orange peel into a crackling fire for a delightful fragrance.

If you're short on table space, an old-fashioned wooden ironing board makes a sturdy sideboard. Just adjust it to a convenient height, add a pretty table runner, and set out the food...
come and get it!

Simple garnishes dress up main dishes all year 'round!
Fresh mint sprigs add coolness and color to
summertime dishes, while rosemary sprigs and
cranberries add a festive touch to holiday platters.

A large oval picture frame with flat glass makes a smart serving tray. Slip family photos or postcards under the glass to personalize.

Set up a framed menu to let everyone know that delicious dishes like Great Grandmother's Pot Roast and Aunt Betty's Pudding Cake await!

Why not host an old-fashioned game night?
All you need are a stack of favorite board games and
some yummy snacks. Pick up some whimsical prizes
from a nearby dollar store...fun for all ages!

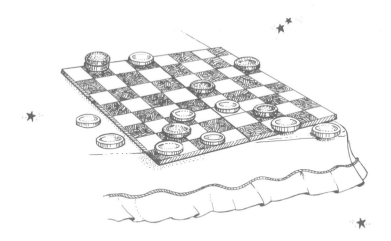

Add some vintage flair to your buffet by placing gently used game boards under your serving dishes. Check the closet for forgotten games or pick some up at yard sales. Cover with self-adhesive clear plastic for wipe-clean ease.

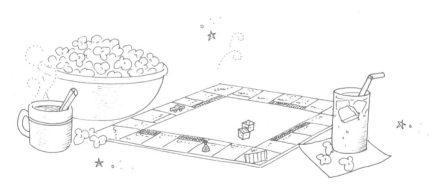

Hosting a dinner party? Stack a few cookies
at each place setting and tie up with
gingham ribbon...a sweet surprise
for each guest.

Package homemade goodies like fudge, peanut brittle
and spiced nuts in snack-sized sacks. Set several in
a basket by the door so guests have a yummy
treat to take home.

Scooped-out mini rounds of bread are just right for individual servings of soups, stews and salads. And the best part...no dishes to wash!

Hollowed-out fruits make refreshing salad servers. Try grapefruits or pineapples...toss the fruit with a yummy honey dressing.

Peppers make garden-fresh servers for catsup, relish and mustard! Just cut a slice off the bottom so they'll sit flat.

Just for fun, use a pumpkin as a soup tureen. An all-white Lumina pumpkin or a plump green and orange Cinderella pumpkin make the prettiest presentations!

Need a little glow for your dinner party? If you don't have a dimmer on your dining room light switch, try replacing the bulbs in your light fixture with a lower wattage pink or golden yellow bulb. Add a few sparkling candles on the table for a warm glow that fills the room.

For the quickest-ever candlelit atmosphere, set several lighted tea lights on the table and top them with metal cheese graters. They'll cast the same twinkling glow as pierced tin lanterns.

Add some shimmer to the party with a simple strand of lights. Decorate the table with a string of white lights folded inside a sheer table runner or strip of fabric. Sparkly!

You're never too old for a tea party! Make
iced cookies or sugar-dusted cakes and fill dainty cups
with soothing chamomile tea...a delightful way for
Grandma to spend an afternoon with her granddaughters.

Teacups & saucers can be had for a song at tag sales. Start a collection with a single theme...pink roses, blue forget-me-nots or whatever strikes your fancy.

What could be more perfect for a tea party than tea roses? Float tea rose blossoms in shallow glass bowls filled with water, or arrange them in single-color or mixed bouquets all around the house.

WELCOME

Having a neighborhood gathering to welcome a new
family? Be sure to give the newcomers a local map so
finding the grocery store, pharmacy, vet and post office
is easy. Have all the neighbors jot down their
favorite fun places to visit, too.

BLESS OUR HoME

Every house where love abides and
friendship is a guest, is surely home,
and home sweet home,
for there the heart can rest.

–Henry Van Dyke

Keep a big roll of wide white freezer paper
on hand for casual get-togethers...party tables
can be covered in a snap and the paper
can be tossed out afterwards.

Stock up on festive party napkins, candles and table decorations at holiday sales. Tuck them away in a big box...you'll be all set to turn any simple get-together into a party.

Welcome to the Party

Invite friends over for a casual potluck supper. What a wonderful way to try new recipes!

Make it easy for guests to mingle and chat...set up food at several tables instead of one big party buffet. Place hot foods on one table, chilled foods on another, sweets on yet another.

Bring a whole new look to your tables by arranging some oversized cloth napkins across the table.

Be sure to have some plastic containers and labels on hand to send everyone home with leftovers...if there are any!

Host a family reunion this year! Plan a full day of activities...horseshoe toss, softball games, three-legged races and lots of catching up! Dust off the picnic tables, load them up with simple, down-home favorites, share recipes and memories and take lots of pictures.

It's a challenge to keep foods chilled on a hot, sunny day when everyone is opening and closing the cooler to get cold drinks. Make it easy...pack one cooler with beverages and another with meats, salads and other perishable foods.

For an affordable get-together, invite friends over
for "just desserts!" Offer two to three simple
homebaked desserts like a cobbler, a layered cake
and a fruit pie, with a steamy pot of coffee
and an assortment of teas...they'll love it!

Pamper your coffee lovers with fresh cream, raw cane sugar and shakers of cinnamon and cocoa. Offer whipped cream for a special treat!

Tea lovers will appreciate selecting from herbal, black or green varieties, along with fresh lemon and honey.

Sparkly fairy lights for the garden...wrap tiny glass jars with craft wire to form hangers and add some colored glass beads. Tuck in votive candles and hang from low branches.

Wrap sandwiches for your garden party in wax paper and tie with a length of gingham ribbon. Serve them in a favorite basket lined with a vintage tea towel.

Headed outside for a backyard party? Grab a
wicker garden caddy...fill it up with napkins,
condiments and everything you need!

Invite friends over for a Salad Supper on a day that's too hot to cook. Ask everyone to bring along a favorite salad. You provide crispy bread sticks or a basket of muffins and a pitcher of iced tea...relax and enjoy!

Serve up summer salad dressings in Mason jars
with a vintage serving spoon...a pretty country touch
for any table.

Fill a large galvanized tub with ice, then
nestle in jars. Everyone can help themselves!

A fun icebreaker for a large gathering of all ages! Divide into two teams...the goal is to line up alphabetically by first names. After 60 seconds, blow a whistle and have each team sound off by name. The team with the most participants in alphabetical order wins!

A good laugh is sunshine in a house.

–William Makepeace Thackeray

Don't have tickets to the big game? Have a tailgate party anyway! Soak up the atmosphere by going to a local high school pep rally or pre-game party. Wear the team colors and cheer them on.

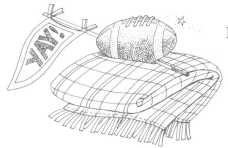

Bring the football field right to your tailgate! Line the truck bed with green outdoor carpeting...easily found at a do-it-yourself hardware store.

Serve up hot & tasty sandwiches at your next tailgating party...right out of a slow cooker! Plug it into a power inverter that uses your car battery to power appliances.

Don't forget finger foods for the kids...tortilla pinwheels and mini pigs-in-a-blanket are great for little tailgaters.

Welcome your neighbors for breakfast or brunch with
steaming mugs of coffee and frosty glasses of juice or milk
Serve morning favorites buffet-style...what a fun way
to enjoy each other's company!

Add a cereal station...pitchers of icy-cold milk
paired with a variety of cereals and fruit are sure
kid-pleasers. You can even have packets of
instant oatmeal on hand.

If the weather is nice, take the party outdoors! Serve breakfast treats on cheery blue and white dishes arranged on homespun placements. Tuck a bouquet of sunflowers in a Mason jar for old-fashioned charm.

Host an Italian potluck. Ask each guest to bring
something to add to the platter...cheeses,
marinated tortellini, olives of all kinds. Delicious!

Create a cozy Italian restaurant feel for your get-together. Toss a red & white checked tablecloth over the table, light drip candles in empty bottles and add a basket of garlic bread.

If you're planning a family get-together,
decorate your table to bring back childhood memories.
Glue photocopies of old family photos to heavy
paper for personalized table centerpieces.

vite the musicians in the family to entertain
your reunion! Whether it's bluegrass fiddle,
assical piano or the guitar,
ur family is sure to enjoy
stening and singing along.

OUR
Reunion

Everyone loves to exchange
recipes at family get-togethers.
Drop a note in the mail ahead
of time asking everyone to jot
theirs down and make lots of
extra copies to share!

Invite friends over for an old-fashioned candy-making party! Pull taffy or stir up some chocolate fudge...you'll have a sweet time together.

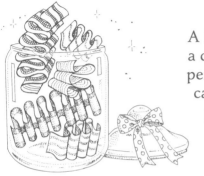

A little candy-making hint:
a cold, sunny winter day is
perfect weather for making
candy. Homemade candy
prepared on a rainy or
humid day may not
set up properly.

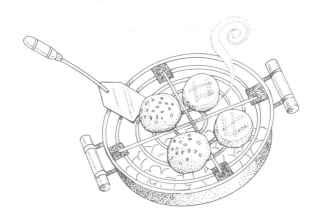

Hosting a barbecue will guarantee a big turnout of
friends & neighbors! Load grills with chicken, ribs,
brats, burgers and hot dogs, then ask guests to bring
a favorite side dish or dessert to share. Add some
yard games and everyone's a winner!

Set up a table in a shady spot and set out a variety of barbecue sauces, spreads, condiments, seasonings, breads, buns and rolls. Friends can pick their favorite combinations or try something new.

For take-home gifts, fill Mason jars with your own special savory sauce. Tie on a recipe card and a BBQ brush with a bit of jute...your guests will love it!

Cooking for a crowd? Roasting meats can easily
be doubled in a large slow cooker. Add only
half again as much seasoning, not twice
as much...otherwise flavors may be too strong.

Slow-cookers make family reunion dinners
so easy! While dinner cooks, families can enjoy a
game of baseball, croquet or hide & seek, or just sit
in the shade catching up with one another.

After a sizzling barbecue meal, cool off with
an assortment of frosty drinks! Keep them cool
by filling a small kiddie pool with lots of
crushed ice. Oh-so refreshing.

Old shoes and old friends are best.

–*Proverb*

Make your gatherings fit your home. Have a tiny dining area but a roomy patio or yard? Plan to invite friends over when you can serve casual meals outdoors.

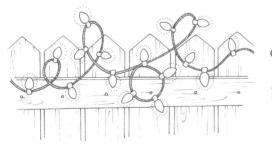

Attach a strand of coolburning light bulbs to the underside of a patio table umbrella or along a fence to create an enchanting effect.

Setting the table for a garden party? Use large terra-cotta saucers lined with glass plates for serving dinner and new hand-held garden tools for fun salad servers. Short lengths of hose wrapped in circles become whimsical garden placemats!

Invite family & friends to an Unbirthday Party. Serve everyone's favorite foods, wear party hats, play games like Pin the Tail on the Donkey and have a silly gift for each person to unwrap. Everyone is sure to have a delightful time!

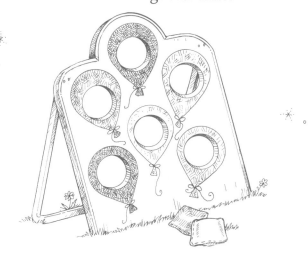

Dost thou love life?
Then waste not time,
for time is the stuff that
life is made of.

–Benjamin Franklin

Hosting a cookie & punch party is an easy way to entertain! Cookies can be baked in advance and frozen. The day before guests arrive, mix up a punch to refrigerate and remove cookies from the freezer. At party time, just pour punch into a punch bowl, arrange cookies on trays and greet your friends.

Nestle mini cookies in paper cupcake liners
and arrange in a shallow box for a pretty
buffet table presentation.

Host a cookie swap...a terrific way to get a variety of yummy cookies! Invite six to eight friends and ask them to bring a half dozen cookies for each guest. Everyone takes as many home...yum!

Create a sweet keepsake for cookie swap guests...ask guests to send their recipes to you before the party and make copies for everyone. Put them together in a little booklet so everyone can take one home.

A lasting memory of the fun...send guests home with a jar of homemade frosting or a new sugar shaker to add to their baking collections.

A neighborhood pie party is a tasty way to get together with nearby friends! Invite everyone to tie on an apron and bring their best-loved pie to share, along with extra copies of the recipe. Enjoy some new-to-you flavors along with great conversation!

A treasured collection of pie birds make "tweet" placecard holders! Just cut out cardstock, print on names, then nestle them right in the beaks. So cute!

Spice up your meal planning with some new ideas when you host a recipe swap party! Invite friends to bring a favorite casserole along with enough recipe cards for each guest. While everyone is enjoying the potluck of scrumptious food, collect the recipe cards, make a stack for everyone, and hand out when the party is over.

For a party favor they'll "flip" over, copy
family favorite recipes onto 4"x6" index cards
and slip into a mini photo album.

Callie's Potato Casserole
10-3/4 can cream mushroom Soup
1 - cup milk
4-6 Redskin Potatoes, boiled, pealed
1/2 cup green pepper, chopped
1/2 cup onion, chopped

salt and pepper
1 cup shredded cheddar Cheese
over →

When guests are coming for brunch, a little kitchen prep
the night before is really helpful. Whisk up eggs for
scrambling, stir together dry ingredients for waffles and
lay out tableware ahead of time...in the morning, just tie on
your prettiest apron and you'll be a relaxed hostess!

*Happiness always looks small
while you hold it in your hands,
but let it go and you learn at once
how big and precious it is.*

–Maxim Gorky

A fireside cookout can be as near as your own backyard! Gather friends and family and enjoy the crisp fall air. Play touch football, toast marshmallows, tell ghost stories, jump into a pile of leaves...be a kid again!

Break out Grandma's great old cast-iron cookware (or your own!) and cook up a tasty meal outdoors. Cast iron takes a little while to heat up, but once heated, it cooks evenly...perfect for an uneven heat source like a campfire. Don't forget the s'mores for dessert!

Cookie cutters make the cutest napkin rings...what fun take-home gifts for guests.

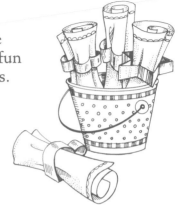

Stack up each guest's place setting, then tie it up with ribbon and tuck fresh blossoms in the knot...everyone will feel like they're sitting down to a special gift!

Emily

Save the memories! Be sure to take pictures
at your gathering and share copies with friends
as a thank-you for coming. Or use an instant
camera for added fun...give pictures
to guests on their way home.

Relax and serve your next dinner party family-style...set large platters of food right on the table so guests can help themselves.

For buffets or dinner parties, roll up flatware in
colorful napkins, tie with ribbon bows and stack
in a flat basket. Even kids can help with this well in
advance of the party...one less last-minute task!

The simplest way to plan a party...choose a theme!

Whether it's Fiesta Night, 1950s Diner or Hawaiian Luau, a theme suggests appropriate dishes, decorations and music. It gives guests something fun on their calendars to look forward to!

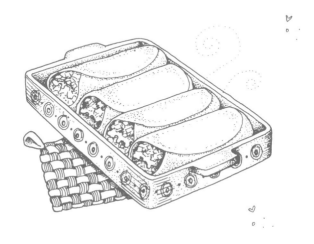

For a Mexican-inspired fiesta, dress up the table in
south-of-the-border style...arrange colorful woven blankets,
sombreros and tissue paper flowers around the room!

All kinds of colorful, fun items for table decorating, serving and party favors are as near as your neighborhood dollar store.

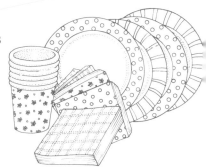

Have fun with party invitations...hand deliver the details rolled up in a small glass bottle or write them on the "tail" of a party blower.

Another fun way to invite guests over...fill bouquets of balloons with helium and write the who, what and where party information on each with a permanent pen. Hand deliver or tie securely to doorknobs with lengths of curling ribbon.

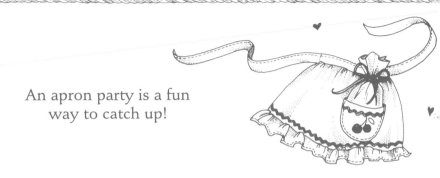

An apron party is a fun way to catch up!

Invite your best girlfriends to tie on their frilliest vintage aprons and join you in the kitchen to whip up a favorite dish. Sit down and enjoy dinner together...and don't forget to snap a couple photos

The ornament of a house
is the friends who frequent it.

–Ralph Waldo Emerson

Serving lunch at a kids' backyard gathering?
Plastic flying discs make fun plates...great
take-home party favors too!

Embellish paper cups with fancy touches kids big and
little will love! Faux jewels, stickers, wax seals
and ribbon easily turn paper cups from
the party store into something special.

Organize a block party and bring neighbors together for some fun! First, you'll need to check with your local police department to see if you need a permit, then set a date. Ask each family to bring a main dish for their family, plus a dish to share. Gather together several grills so everyone can cook without missing any of the fun!

Indian Summer is the perfect time of year for a neighborhood block party...the weather is still warm and fall foliage is gorgeous. Use hay bales to set up some quick tables!

Bring along bubble wands, jump ropes and
squirt guns to your next outing...grownups will
have as much fun as kids and you'll get some
great candid snapshots!

Call friends and enjoy an impromptu summer afternoon together. Serve a cold pitcher of iced tea and soak up some sun while you're catching up.

*The greatest gift of life
is friendship, and I have
received it.*

–Hubert H. Humphrey

Our Story

ck in 1984, we were next-door neighbors raising our families in the little town of elaware, Ohio. Two moms with small children, we were looking for a way to do what e loved and stay home with the kids too. We had always shared a love of home cooking d making memories with family & friends and so, after many a conversation over the ckyard fence, **Gooseberry Patch** was born.

e put together our first catalog at our kitchen tables, enlisting the help of our loved ones erever we could. From that very first mailing, we found an immediate connection with any of our customers and it wasn't long before we began receiving letters, photos and cipes from these new friends. In 1992, we put together our very first cookbook, compiled m hundreds of these recipes and, the rest, as they say, is history.

rd to believe it's been over 25 years since those kitchen-table days! From that original little **ooseberry Patch** family, we've grown to include an amazing group of creative folks who e cooking, decorating and creating as much as we do. day, we're best known for our homestyle, family-friendly okbooks, now recognized as national bestsellers.

ne thing's for sure, we couldn't have done it without our ends all across the country. Each year, we're honored to n thousands of your recipes into our collectible cookbooks. ur hope is that each book captures the stories and heart all of you who have shared with us. Whether you've en with us since the beginning or are just discovering us, elcome to the **Gooseberry Patch** family!

JoAnn & Vickie

Visit our website anytime
www.gooseberrypatch.com
1·800·854·6673

Since 1992, we've been publishing our bestselling cookbooks for every kitchen and every meal of the day! With hundreds of budget-friendly recipes using ingredients you already have on hand, their lay-flat binding makes them easy to use. Each is filled with hand-drawn artwork and plenty of personality.

Have a taste for more?

We created our official Circle of Friends so we could fill everyone in on the latest scoop at once. Visit us online to join in the fun and discover free recipes, exclusive giveaways and much more!

www.gooseberrypatch.com

Join Our Circle of Friends

Find Gooseberry Patch in Your Neighborhood

f Find us on Facebook

You Tube

t Follow us on twitter

Read Our Blog